THE FIVE PETALS OF ELDERFLOWER

The Five Petals of Elderflower

Poems

For Caron

Thank you for your enthusiasm for my poetry.

ANGELA TOPPING

Angela Topping

January 2018

RED SQUIRREL PRESS

First published in the UK in 2016 by Red Squirrel Press
www.redsquirrelpress.com
Reprinted 2017

Edited by Elizabeth Rimmer
www.burnedthumb.co.uk

Designed and typeset by Gerry Cambridge
www.gerrycambridge.com

Cover picture credit: © <a href='http://www.123rf.com/profile_
megapixelina'>megapixelina / 123RF Stock Photo</a>

A CIP catalogue record for this book is available from the
British Library.

ISBN: 978 1 910437 39 1

Red Squirrel Press is committed to a sustainable future.
This book is printed in the UK by Imprint Digital
using Forest Stewardship Council certified paper.
www.imprintdigital.co.uk

Contents

That day she put our heads together,
Fate had her imagination about her,
Your head so much concerned with outer,
Mine with inner, weather.

—*Robert Frost*

The disorder of gulls in a pleasure of words,
the glint of the mullet, the pigness of pigs.

—*Matt Simpson*

The Five Petals of Elderflower

With the odd number five strange nature's laws
Plays many freaks nor once mistakes the cause.
—John Clare

I

Enter through its centre of five petals
past the crown of stamens like matches
slide down the green stem, landing with legs
either side of the junction between stalks.
Now you are surrounded by flowers.
Soak up the hum—you are at one with lace.
Sleep now, as in fresh sheets, soothed
by the sun, head in blossom, a perfumed lullaby,
leaves far below to catch you if you fall.
But you will not fall: the petioles enmesh.
Your cheek is on your mother's breast,
the flowers are sweet milk. Rock-a-bye.

II

This tree is elder. It's safe. With the blossoms
we can make elderflower champagne
with the berries, elderberry wine.
Put your nose into it. Yes, it's a good scent.
If it smells like cat's pee, so will your champagne.
So we don't pick those. This tree is fine.
Hold this bag open while I cut some.
We don't want to drop any—
see how easily each flower head can come away.
There's lots of stories about this tree. Some say
it's Faerie, but your mum knows more about that.
I say it's very good to use. But we mustn't
take all the blooms from one tree or there'll be
no berries, neither for us nor birds.

III

The smell is buzzing in my head, as we walk
down the night lane, away from the heated air
of the pub where friends spilled onto the car park.
We whisper as we pass sleeping cottages—
can't even see the elder, just smell it, as the lane
becomes a funnel of scents and fuzzy leaves.
I'm giddy, stumbling; now there is no-one to see
you take my hand. We cannot even see each other.
The flowers smell of sex, of lust, foreign tongues to us.
Too soon the lane opens out into streetlights,
pavements, cars. You drop my hand. The scent
is left behind, pollened on memory.

IV

Elderflowers sing jazz, each petalled phrase
plays another variation on the last.
Its saxophone voice rises above twanged strings
of cello and double bass, holding the melody
as it flies high. Notes dance round our feet:
we wade in sound. It's a five bar blues,
scrolls of baroque, rising like smoke, tasting champagne.
White is not white, is green and cream and ivory.
And it sings the blues.

V

By its five textures: the rough underside of leaves
and the smooth front, the strong stem, thinner wands
of stalks, and cobbly lace of blossom like slubbed silk.
By its green taste, its umbrella canopy,
by the cushion of blooms each with five petals.
By these things, I swear to remember you.

Seed-Time

Plants are resourceful. They try every method
to scatter their seed: dandelion parachutes,
sycamore wing nuts, jester's crowns of columbine,
poppy's wooden boxes that rattle like maracas,
rosebay willow herb's cotton graffiti everywhere.

How unprepossessing the scattered seeds are:
black pepper specks, dried husks, pips hiding
in the apple's secret chambers, or buried in grapes,
sunflower seeds like moths' wings, schoolgirl plaits
of wheat ears, all herringbone and gold.

Strange packets of genetic coding, humble bundles:
instructions for oaks, copper beeches, aspens,
delphiniums, foxgloves, primroses or thyme.
Nurtured in soil's darkness, by leaf mould and decay
and worms' slow stomachs, by luck and skywater.

Winter's blankness proves them, until invisible threads
pull new shoots from earth, whether for a single summer
or a tree's long endurance. They take hold and flourish
on bombsites, verges, in fields, wherever they can thrive,
spreading their empires of greens and pinks and blues.

Spawn

All night the frogs purr in the pond.
Their insistent lust to procreate
has driven them into suburbia.

They chill out in balletic poses,
just visible, their slack heads poking out,
their legs hanging amongst cool fronds.

We wait for milky tapioca of frogspawn
to cling in cloudy globs
to last year's iris stalks.

Each morning we shoo away the heron,
hover anxiously when ducks
descend, play chase on the water.

We report daily progress to each other
and long after the parents have
hopped off, we peer into the pond's eye

anxious as midwives, while the crotchets
jiggle away from the stave and begin
to make music. Months later

every frog, silk among green silk,
is greeted as though it brought
a gift of coins in its pursed mouth.

Sparrow

Passer, deliciae meae puellae
                              —Catullus

When wind and earth joined together
to make the sparrow, they set
its toy heart flickering,
its small feet clicking. The breast
was made from speckled foam,
the wings painted with colours
left over from other creations:
burnt sienna, cafe latte, sludge.

Although the bird's beauty
was doubtful, it could weave in
and out of hedges, eaves and thatch.
The voice was nothing special:
a chirrup like a giggle fastened
in its throat like a comedy brooch.

Wind and earth baptised their child.
The first fairy godmother named it *passer,*
the second gave it joy, the third
the greatest gift of all: to be convivial.
The sparrow was a great success,
beloved of a poet's paramour, able to
hop into human habitations unafraid.

Spoken Cartography

What is the riddle of this hill?
It tells of secret graves, of bones.
It sings of granite, rabbits' homes.
Records of battles are scribbled on grass.
Blood fattens bulbs for spring.

What is the legend of this tree?
The heartwood knows important things.
Its shade is where the lovers sighed;
its branches where thrushes feed their young.
The oak means ships and England's pride.

What is the codex of the sky?
Its meaning changes by the hour.
Its tongue no-one can understand.
Its daily dialectic tells one truth:
nothing is definite except the dark.

Autumn Boggling

In homage to Britain's lesser known village names

All along the yedge, the papple grows
thick with parva attracted by pollen.
It spreads purple as framboo.

I love to sit up here, watching for asloss,
hearing the yocken call on the ferwig breeze.
At pimpernel, the sun turns carburn

blending the sky ink pink and gold.
I often see an abinger, hovering below.
Time to set off for home, for coggles

by the fireside, stamping up the path
with my basket of cambo, at peace.
I ease off boots, dump them in the stublish,

open the door to the sound of the goomebell,
chiming the hour, in time for bablock and esh
as outside, whapload comes creeping.

Welcome to Royston Vasey

Bab's taxi lurches down the high street, past
boarded-up Fleur de Lys with its gladioli ghosts,
round the Roundabout Zoo, watched by the angel
with his laurel crown, to collect a stranger
from the trembling train. Down at the job centre
Pauline clutches the pens, her only friends,
as jobseekers shuffle off to Dick Fisher's:
a flutter on the three o-clock passes dull afternoons.

In school they are doing Geography: lines and lines
and lines on a map, chanting places they will never visit.
In the back bedroom of the Local Shop
David's flicking through comics. Gorged on
sweets and squirrel, he howls for a mate.
Evenings find Chinnery and Briss at the Mason's Arms
propping up the bar, fingers sticky from their trades.
This is their town; they want no trouble here.

The Palace Pictures is no palace but the teens pile in,
counting the days till they can get away, from parents
intoning *in this house*, all rules and jangling keys.
What's all this shouting? More strangers will come.
New Road. The Local Shop will soon be an Asda,
the Palace a bingo hall. There will be no going back.

Wirral Way

By redshank, by curlew, by peregrine falcon,
by shore and by field in the path of the trains
whose rattle was stoppered and silenced forever
when rails were pulled up and sleepers destroyed;
past Parkgate and Gayton and Heswall and down
to the beach where the Dee never tires in its flow;
by tides of the river, by dogs chasing children,
by high clouds and breezes and rock pools with crabs;
along backs of gardens, along high green hedges,
tramp along gravel by hawthorn and birch;
by willow herb, cow parsley, butterflies, dragonflies,
lapwing and skylark to West Kirby caffs;
by sun on the water, a bolt of bright satin
to Hilbre Island the home of the seals.

Three Views at Ty Newydd

I

The fireweed, rosebay willow herb,
colonises everything, its feathery tufts
signal the release of assertive seed
on waste ground, bombsite, margin lands.
At least it's alive, at least something's home.

II

From where I stand, the indifferent sea
appears in air, smudging horizons,
its secrets untold. It whispers of them
but words will not be caught.

These strange margins and borderlands
are of themselves, not humankind.
The sleeping sea could with one push
rub out these scattered farms.

III

Turning through 360 degrees
I see primordial forest
pines, ivy ascending birches, holly,
sea, sea, sea. Then back
to house and garden, the small fixings
and bright colours of human craft:
two worlds, the door between
still ajar.

Studying the Travel Question

Travel can be dangerous and adventurous
declares the question we discuss
in A level classes. You're not kidding.

Today, I risked my life, driving through
February snow, still falling, deadly white
on motorway and screen.

Fields and trees of enticing loveliness
tempted me to stop, park the car, set out
in work suit and unsuitable shoes.

Robert Frost spoke in my mind, dark and deep.
One day there will be no promises to keep.

Coniston Water from Brantwood

For Geraldine Green

Up here, through pine branches, I see
it's not the sort of day for me to venture out.

Below me slate steps, slippery with rain
lead back down the grey road.

In parkas and over-trousers,
groups of walkers damply gather.

Waves on the swelling mere are Vs
like flocks of birds drawn by a child.

Boats are tethered; even the trees
are doing their best to stand proud.

On the far side, white cottages hunker
like dogs, blurred in the downpour.

Across the Water, mist covers fell tops,
settling in for the night like a shroud.

My Own Address

This oak roof comforts me whenever
Mother drives the hoover monster close;
I see its snarling metal teeth. The house is
my own address, my damask walls.

Under this table, I have kissed feet:
they are gone now, these people I love.
It's just me and my doll, and she
is no company at all. Her eyes are empty.

When my mother's house is full again
I will emerge, be given sweets. My daddy,
home from work, will invite me
to sit in my other place, the house he makes

between his back and his chair's back.
I do not know why hiding is needed
nor when I'm sad I go under the bed
where balls of grey dust scut like rabbits.

Are You Sitting Comfortably?

For John Shuttleworth

Are you sitting comfortably? Then I'll begin.
BBC voice, immaculate, the speech I was made for.
Not the dragged-out dragged-up hometown vowels,
first-up best-dressed accent mum despised,
but correctness, buffed and polished as our table.

The music rolled its *r*s and washed over us.
Mother washing up in the kitchen, and I—
daily surprised at the treat of story from the brown box—
gathered all my people, rounded up,
from abandonment, to be drilled in line,
strict size order, with me, their leader, at one end
descending to the smallest teddy, in time

for fifteen minutes' absorption before Faure's Dolly Suite
spread its sleepy honey round the shabby room.
This was my order of service, my litany, my prayer,
My mum's aspiration for me, to speak properly,
to take my place in the world, with a tongue
fit to command. No woolly-back drawl for me.

Until I went to school in Liverpool, caught
a twang of Scouse and fell into belonging
like a warm bath, all suds and consonants,
vowels squashed by a river's weight, by all
the speakers who'd flowed in on Mersey tides.
And now at last am sitting comfortably with myself.

Topical Iodine

Blue as school ink with rumours of purple,
medicinal perfume to scent our scrapes,
blossoming on skin, bestowed by crisp nurses.

A bleeding knee was dabbed with sapphire drops,
its sting soon forgiven, as Rorschach blots
spread their magic, dripped into white socks.

How many times I fell in the yard
to exchange dull assembly for a walk alone
through streets silent of school clatter, fizzing rhymes

forming themselves in my mouth, the copper of
rainy pavements leading to sky-blue railings,
stone steps, wedged-open clinic doors:

antiseptic spells, where there were no bullies,
no screaming teachers, but a hushed routine,
lace-ups squeaking on polished floors.

I tried words for size, like *tincture* and *chemical*,
words I was too young to spell, though their rhythms
chimed in my ear, saved up like cajoled coins.

My iodine days, those blue forgotten mornings,
now obsolete, half a century away from here,
scented like parma violets, sweet on my tongue.

Cradle Catholic

For years I dreamed of leaving
but the pull was strong: so many
memories of being moved and loved,
of lit candles and swelling organ music,
bright words glittering.

As holy bells warned us to raise
bowed heads, adore, we'd chant
Glory, glory, glory, Lord God of Hosts.
On long walks home from church,
I'd mither for the words of hymns
before reading unlocked my first poetics.

What gorgeousness was there?
the year's calendar shone in vestments:
silks of purple, green and white
embroidered with gold thread
by cloistered nuns, the stitches prayers.
Words like *ciborium* and *monstrance,*
biretta and *stole,* delighted the ear.

Incense mingled with damp wool.
The congregation intoned as one:
lamb of God, ave, womb—
a mysterious place our Lord came from.
I thought it meant the sound of voices
moving together like water.

The round bread, baked by holy sisters,
was God's eye, scouring secret hearts.
The priest placed it on stuck-out tongues
where the wafer slowly melted.
The palate's ribbed roof was tabernacle.

Angels clustered round the altar. I thought
I could hear their wing beats. I offered
all my sorrows up to Jesus, as I'd been taught.
But this was my mother's God. Without her
I had to find my own ways of knowing.

When Widnes was in Lancashire
and I was in Widnes

I climbed my childhood scrapheap,
finding footholds on old prams,
rusting bikes; reddened metal
that slid under my feet and hands.

My fingers stretched to scrape the sky,
head buoyed up with words I'd claimed
understood but couldn't say
from all the books I'd hefted home.

The small town couldn't hold me. I
was Alice in Wonderland, stuck
in the White Rabbit's house, drunk
on grow-me potion, glugging it down.

I was waiting for the wind to change,
to tread the yellow brick road
journeying beyond myself, beyond the town
beyond the people I had known.

The Transporter's comforting boards
upstaged by the dizzy arc of a bridge:
a monochrome rainbow, an exit sign
spanning the horizon, lit up in chemical dark.

From downriver, mermaids called me
to where the Mersey became the sea,
a gull-haunted strait with looming ships
to New Brighton, Éire, The Caribbean.

The Visited

How mum came to know them I never knew;
their only friend, she took them food parcels,
ran errands, offered chatter like coins,
and sometimes clothes. And always, she took me,
as though a child's face could give them hope.

At mum's knock, they'd open doors a scared
two inches, then wider. Straight in from the street
to rooms stuffed with knick-knacks:
wax blooms and dead birds under a dusty dome;
bronze stags; crinoline girls, and cranberry glass.

Remnants of servants from big houses,
not encouraged to marry, they retired
to nurse decaying parents in rented terraces,
then folded sheets over their dead faces.

Behind yellowed lace, they slept downstairs,
bedrooms an Everest away and bitter cold.
easier not to have to use the chamber pot,
nothing to go upstairs for, anyway.

Everything about them scared me:
The staleness of their breath, their skin
engraved with dirt, and most of all
the thought of one day being them.

They Pose Together

The mother's in black: embroidered cross-over jacket
pinned with watch and brooch. At her throat
squats a cameo, knotted hands display a wedding ring.
Her skirt is stiff as buckram. Practical black lace-ups,
polished like lumps of coal, show under her dress.
Whitening hair is gathered back, unsmiling mouth
gives nothing away. Her back is upright in the chair.

The daughter perches on the chair's arm, balanced,
one foot tucked behind, waiting to launch into a waltz.
White shoes and stockings, lawn dress delicate as paper.
She has her mother's cheeks, without the fold and crease;
matching dimples in their chins. Her smile opens
on pearl-white teeth, lips softly parting.
No clip can restrain her dark curls where they spring.

They are hinged together, one a negative of the other.
One looks back on fulfilment, widowed now, growing
towards beeswax candles, hushed voices, drawn curtains—
a froth of white lace still at throat and wrist; the daughter
waiting for the yet to come. For this studio photograph
they are stitched together, a book bound dos á dos.
It has always been this way with mothers and daughters.

Noost

'Pocket Noost' by Douglas Robertson, a miniature landscape in a tin

I have moored a small boat
in a sheltered Shetland bay.
Your name is painted starboard.
The wood is bleached by salt;
oars stowed under the bench,
ready for you anytime.

Push it into the water, step aboard.
Row where your will takes you,
into the green, towards
distant mountains you long to climb.
The cool blubber of waves
laps and sucks in rhythm
as steady as your heartbeat.
Sea birds thicken the air as you beach.
You are drunk on sea smells,
damp scent of mermaid's purse.

    This is the life you were born for.
    Not that narrow place, where you are
    pinned like a bug in a specimen drawer.

Carry my gift in your pocket.
When you open this rusty tin:
the gulls' shriek is deafening,
water moves and tumbles,
your feet are bare on ribbed sand,
your hands calloused; the sun
is on your back, soothing, soothing.

When you close the lid again
that world winks out, is gone
but stays within; sea, mountains, sky,
that place of quiet I bring you.

Formby Sands

This beach is not for sunbathing,
not at this time of year.
Inland, birds may sing
and hawthorn's pink tips
froth in the woods, but here

wind makes new partings
in my hair, blows shell-grit
ground by sea-roiling
into my mouth and eyes.
The dunes have swallowed you.

I wade through shifting sand
which sucks and ripples
as I try to follow.
Words are ripped from my mouth.
Where are you? I flounder

think I'll never find you again
scale sand hills close to crying,
not that anyone would hear me
in this banshee place
of screaming gusts and gulls.

When we find each other
between dips and rises, your calling
and mine, things we dare not say
rise like distant waves,
glitter in cold spring light.

Wenlock Edge Walk

It's now Eastertide.
Catkins are springing in the woods.
Six weeks since we met:
there are so many things to tell
we wear out the day.

You help me from stiles,
let me clutch your arm's hard knots
on the steep descents.
This is walking on the edge—
my joke, your laughter.

June day in Colyton

For Jan Dean

On this duck-egg blue morning
even seagulls keep their voices down.
The whirr of pigeons' wings ruffles the air.

We stroll sloping streets, gazing
as summer flowers punch colour on walls
white as china or oatmeal antique linen.

Butterflies flicker, making no sound
as they tip wings from bloom to bloom.
No need for conversation between us,

we match step for step, dreamily.
Each house has its own story to tell,
each door keeps its own secrets.

Stigliano

In this Tuscan July heat
we who are never idle
are having to learn
how to do nothing.

Siena's high stone walls
trap warm air; even the shade
is baked hot, a stone oven.
Visits there exhaust us.

In Palazzo Stigliano
we alternate shaded seats
with indoor chill,
lurk by the fan.

Skin slick with factor 40,
we dress in loose linens,
go swimming just to feel normal,
make the simplest meals.

Museums and galleries keep
their secrets for a cooler visit.
We sip icy wine, scan
sunflower fields from hilltop

watch the sun sink,
lay our backs against stone,
retreat into the shepherd's house,
sleep under a single sheet.

Company on the Road

I was lost
after a diversion
and in the dark
driving home
from a poetry reading;
you came
as though
death were
no bar
to keep
me company
not by speech—
beyond you now—
but by your scent,
that musk
of clean sweat
I'd known you by
alive
and a sudden warmth
ran through me
like a flame.

New Year

It's poor weather for walking: cold, dank.
But you needed the quiet of these woods
where ivy glosses the path's edge
and frosted leaves lie slippy underfoot.

Rime freezes mittens on the bridge rail.
We speak of things that do not matter,
emerge from trees into a clearing
where a sycamore spreads its shade.

When snow falls, it will change everything
make a page for you to write on.

Apple

I want to be an apple:
so fresh my pips rattle.
Not a Golden Delicious
or Granny Smith
but a Worcester Pearmain,
green with one red cheek.
When I was young I was all blossom
now I'm ripe, my flesh crisp, juicy,
so tender each scrap can be eaten.
I am at my best. Enjoy me now.

Ichthyolatry

He loved the calico skin of the koi,
her scarlet daubs. The tail flexed
like a ballerina's legs. She lifted
her sucking mouth from the water.

Each night he visited. His wife's
bullish snores polluted his dreams.
The fish made no demands, she came
clean as pearl in pellucid silence.

Every day, her ivory face glided
in and out of lectures and seminars,
until at last he could pour his whisky,
make pilgrimage to shaded water

where she glowed like a lamp. He'd wait
for her kiss on his fingertips. For her,
he planted purple water lilies.
Soon the nights were no longer enough.

When he began to spend his weekends
face-down, gazing into the pond,
lifting the carp from the water,
his wife's shoulder blades became cleavers.

A koi tattoo now burnishes his skin.
He feels it ripple and remembers how
her underbelly pulsated in his bed,
the nights he held the body of a fish.

Invitation for Tomorrow

Come for breakfast.

We will eat grapes, raspberries and cold meats.
There will be warm croissants just out of the oven,
Roquefort, Port-Salut and White Stilton.
We will drink Buck's Fizz and Blue Mountain Coffee.

Come. My fire is lit.

My sofa is decked with fat cushions and soft throws.
In the company of gold-tooled books
we will talk poetry, and memories, submit
to each other new poems for the winkling of commas.

Stay for the day.

In the afternoon, tired out from talk and laughter,
we'll cuddle up together, take a nap
for on this day there will be no rules. We can say
all the things we could not when we were both alive.

How to Capture a Poem

Look for one at midnight
on the dark side of a backlit angel
or in the space between a sigh

and a word. Winter trees, those
elegant ladies dressed in diamonds
and white fur, may hide another.

Look for the rhythm in the feet
of a waltzing couple one, two, three-ing
in an empty hall, or in the sound

of any heartbeat, the breath of a sleeper,
the bossy rattle of keyboards in offices,
the skittering of paper blown along.

You could find a whole line
incised into stone or scrawled on sky.
Words float on air in buses, are bandied

on street corners, overheard in pubs,
caught in the pages of books, sealed
behind tight lips, marshalled as weapons.

Supposing you can catch a poem,
it won't tell you all it knows. Its voice
is a whisper through a wall, a streak of silk

going by, the scratch of a ghost, the creaks
of a house at night, the sound of the earth
vibrating in spring, with all its secret life.

You have to listen: the poem chooses itself,
takes shape and begins to declare what it is.
Honour the given, else it will become petulant.

When you have done your best,
you have to let it go. Season it with salt
from your body, grease it with oil from your skin.

Release it. It has nothing more to do
with you. You're no more its owner
than you hold the wind. Never expect gratitude.

Bookbinding at The Whitworth

For Lucy May Scofield

The room opens like a secret. Around the table
like place settings, unfamiliar tools beg to be handled.

Paper has grain and thickness matters. We learn to
find its warp and woof, become intimate by touch.

The steps we follow are prayers: fold edge
to edge, smoothe with bone folder, fold and crease

careful not to bruise the tender pages. With awl,
learn to puncture sewing holes, then linen thread

beeswaxed, pulled through and knotted tight.
From the most ordinary of materials, books

wake under our hands: pamphlets, concertinas,
beak books, pages we can turn, small artefacts.

Lucy opens her thirties suitcase, taunts us
with books we cannot hope to make.

Fish and Chips

It's the cracking crisp batter,
a steaming envelope of milky fish:
haddock, cod or skate so recently
leading its salty life in North Sea water.
This nourishment fills all the empty places.

And that's not counting the golden brown
chunks of deep-fried potato, fluffy inside
just like dad used to make (or mum
when he was out at evening mass
because in his credo, chips were not
suitable Sunday food). Nor the soft green
mush of marrowfat peas, throat poultices.

Bring me hot paper parcels from the chippy's
cheerful greasy banter. We will eat them
with wooden forks or fingers, out of doors
in Blackpool, New Brighton or Southport,
on a bench where fresh breezes sting our cheeks,
and hot vinegar is all the comfort we need.

Man with Fishing Rod

'On his holidays' by John Singer Sargent

Relaxing on a stone couch
grey workpants becoming
part of the landscape
instead of stinging factories

white cotton clings like lichen
pure as clean foaming water
gurgling round rocks like soapsuds
away from blackening mills

in his cap fretted flies
twisted by light of worn-out
winter firelight from feathers
hoarded from scatterings in back yards

factory shut down week
utmost absorption
red raw knuckles grasp the rod
leaping silver within his reach.

Lake District Love Song

I have seen this land under snow:
drumlin swarms nestling together,
Geography lessons proved true,
sheep placidly eating and shitting
half-way up fells, shepherds
strolling up steep slopes easily,
their dogs to heel.

I have seen this land under rain:
Grizedale Forest leaves dripping,
damp boots and socks, map
pulping at the creases. I've seen
a bright day turn suddenly chill
as clouds heavy with water
burst over Windermere.

I have seen this land glitter
under bright sun, intensifying
all its green delights, the vale
spread out, a diminutive Eden.
My feet have been immersed
in its mountain becks, crickets
creaking from the furze.

Exiled to the valleys now,
I take my turn round shops,
drink Jennings beer in pubs,
no longer able to manage
even Catbells or Dolly Wagon Pike.
I try to hold the viewfinder
on remembered views, watch
cloud patterns forming on the fells.

Nothing but Rain

The window pane is streaked and spotted.
The beech hedge offers little comfort to birds.
Water puddles in the road, car headlamps sheen.
The bird feeder bobs on the almond branches.

Edward Thomas wrote about rain like this,
that drenched and seeped through fustian uniform.
He sheltered in a shed and heard rain drum
on the corrugated iron room, in such despair

as he'd been able to assuage by tramping
fields and woods where he lived in England.
No such warmth for him now, days or weeks
away from death, in a war that wasted

poets and painters and musicians,
labourers and farm hands, thinkers and doers
as trenches filled with mud and blood.
Even the weather was against them.

Rain is still as wet, and drips into poems
like this one, but each one after his
calls out in fellow feeling, as if his Rain
and ours is the same, as if shelter would come

and safety, and warmth and life, like mine
by this coal fire, time for his English words,
to flock into his mind with feathery lines,
so he could once more sing of birds.

Agnes

Midwood Street, terraces not fit for humans,
is where she's always lived. It's twenty years
since she last climbed the stairs.

Layers of dust stifle outdated ornaments.
Each sloughed-off cell deepens the pall.
Gas lamps are chandeliered with webs.

Her body's a bent stick, wrapped
in a flowery pinny, stained with grease.
Even her voice is a husk, a wisp of dried grass.

Nothing can grow here now. Her skin
is fissured as earth denied its dew,
ingrained dirt highlights every line.

Eggshell eyes are barely blue, faded
with each passing year
of servitude to parents now long dead.

Boyfriends had not been allowed. Each ovum
shrivelled inside, like dried walnuts,
her sex not her own to give.

To this drought her whole life has brought her.
Her purpose ended with Father's final breath,
Mother's last soaping as she laid the body out.

Late Roses

All day we have been working,
side by side in your childhood garden,
lopping shrubs, eradicating brambles
snipping dead heads, yanking weeds.

October roses emerge in vibrant hues:
oranges, golds and crimsons, with thorns
which rip our clothes and flesh.
Their scent is a reward for labour.

Your parents' tangled minds
are clogged with memories, resurfacing
as they approach their nineties.
We have assumed control.

Safe in their new apartment, they cling
to routine, repeat old stories, laugh,
are mostly thankful for our care: roses
late flowering against the dark of winter.

Last Remnants of the Mother Tongue

Llanfairpwllgwyngyllgogerychwyrndrobwllllantysiliogogogoch

The made-up place name was once her party piece.
She found the rhythm and it rolled off her tongue
like a mountain spring from the crags; a girl
from Ffynnongroyw who loved to make others laugh.

Her first language was drummed out of her at school.
English came to be her daily bread not *Cwm Rhondda*,
though a Welsh choir could lift her day, reminding her
of the bard father she loved, her days of mischief at home.

Now from the red cave of her mouth, in her 94th year
white-haired, amongst the scribble of dementia, the last
few scrapings of Welsh words come gentle,
rise again in her before all language is go go gone.

Red Squirrel

after Pascale Petit

Mum lived through both wars
by preserving plastic bags,
collecting milk bottle tops.
She wrote names and dates
on the back of every photo,
stored up stories to save me,
dressed me from jumble sales.

She squirreled away sugar,
stacked bags in her wardrobe
behind Dad's swinging braces
where it set like concrete,
a wall of sweetness;
poor replacement for him
who honeycombed her life.

These days, I think of her
with red pelt and feathery tail.
Scarce and always looked-for,
she leaps up perpendiculars,
on a quest for hazelnuts,
her neat claws clinging
to rough surfaces of trees.

Coffin Texts

Inscribed on the inside
of my cardboard house
while I wait to decompose
in the deep woodland places
where my body can become
leaf mould, food
for oaks and rowans.

No need to paint my image
with a gold face, as if bathed
in sunlight. But let children
colour my coffin with crayons,
doodle me happy.

No guide to the netherworld
but poems to sing me asleep,
poems I have knit into my bones.
This magic is true. A spell
to perfect the body and return it
to the cradle of earth.

On Ghosts

They steal all the teaspoons from the cutlery box,
shrivel the apples with their breath. They make
candle flames flicker when they enter a room,
drink malt whisky straight from the bottle.

They slide up the banister, suck dust from the floor,
sneak into my bedroom and try on clothes,
leave them in a pile on the chair, smelling
of autumn and mothballs. The mirror is misted.

Check the back seat of the car: they prefer
to sit where windows are tinted. Daylight stings.
In the pictures, they sit behind me and whisper,
then slide into the film, inhabit the rainy street.

Like us, they fear the dark, and love fireworks.
They wear Christmas lights like bracelets.
No need to ask who picked the November rose
and scattered the petals all over the lawn.

The Glass Swan

January midnight, a numbness of winter,
not for the first time, I am last awake.
The house is silent except for the hum
of the coal fire, the blue song of the fridge.

All the winters I have been alive, the weather
has been teaching its hard lessons:
those who lived so intensely are gone.
I shall not see them again, though I speak with them

in all the aching chambers of the mind.
Ice has hold of the earth, as those things
which are true but unwelcome, grip memory.
Look at this fire in the hearth, feel it.

Bank it up against the night. It is all we have, these
corporeal things: these candlesticks, this glass swan.

Against the Dark

Earth's little lights flash on and off
and taste the darkness like a draught
of water from the iron trough.

Come saving grace, come holy bough,
come paraclete of flame, that I
may save the glow that warms me now.

This bowl of hills, these singing stones
that circle round about: protect
my midnight flesh and bones.

Let me think these lights shine on
—as stars are there by day and night—
after they are snuffed and gone.

Acknowledgements

'The Five Petals of Elderflower' won first prize in Buzzwords 2013.

Thanks are due to the editors of the following publications where some of these poems first appeared: *Clear Poetry, InterlitQ, Message in a Bottle, Nutshells and Nuggets, Poetry Review, Poetry Scotland, Prole, Southlight, Stand, Stride, The Black Light Engine Room, The Dark Horse, The Examiner, The Fat Damsel, The High Window, The Morning Star, The New Ulster, The North, The Screech Owl, York Mix.*

Some of these poems appeared in the following anthologies: *Double Bill* (Red Squirrel Press, 2014); *Drifting Down the Lane* (Moon and Mountain, 2013); *Great Escapes, Poetry from the Cheshire Prize for Literature* (University of Chester Press, 2014); *My Dear Watson* (Beautiful Dragons Collaborations, 2015); *Sculpted: Poems of the North West* (North West Poets, 2014); *The Poet's Quest for God* (Eyewear, 2016); *Troubles Swapped for Something Fresh* (Salt, 2009).

Thanks are due to Gladstone's Library for awarding me a writer-in-residence post in 2013, during which time some of these poems were first drafted.